Simply Written

Demi-Lea Tilsley

Published by New Generation Publishing in 2020

Copyright © Demi-Lea Tilsley 2020

First Edition

The author asserts the moral right under the Copyright, Designs and Patents Act 1988 to be identified as the author of this work.

All Rights reserved. No part of this publication may be reproduced, stored in a retrieval system or transmitted, in any form or by any means without the prior consent of the author, nor be otherwise circulated in any form of binding or cover other than that which it is published and without a similar condition being imposed on the subsequent purchaser.

ISBN 978-1-80031-429-0

www.newgeneration-publishing.com

ABOUT THE AUTHOR

My name is Demi-Lea Tilsley nee Pearson.

I was born in 1994 and raised in a small town called Hednesford in Staffordshire by my mother Angie & Dad Malcolm. I have one sibling, a younger brother Corey.

I married in 2016 to Adam Tilsley after a long friendship. I spent my school years attending Pye Green Valley Primary and Blake Valley Technology College. I didn't really enjoy studying as my interests lay in outdoors or sports. I trained in Martial arts from an early age, following my father's footsteps. My father was a blackbelt in Karate & Kickboxing and I followed by gaining mine to. I was also a keen football player and played in a couple of local teams.

I grew up in a very close knitted family and enjoyed the family network, spending most of my spare time with my cousins.

I'm now working in health & social care where I'm a deputy manager in a small home for adults who have autism & learning difficulties. I identify as a Christian and attend church regularly.

WHY I WRITE

The reason I started writing poetry was in 2017 I sadly lost my Grandad (Gramps) to cancer. This affected me quite badly as we were very close. I had trouble with my mental health due to this and found it helped to write my thoughts down.

I started writing one, then two and I found I couldn't stop. My imagination just carried on, as thoughts came into my head, I wrote them down. Not all my poems are from personal experience and feelings, sometimes my imagination runs wild and I have to write. Sometimes I'd just people watch, and a poem would spring up, or I could hear a story on the news or read one in a newspaper and it would trigger me to write.

IN LOVING MEMORY OF
BARRIE ROGERS
FOREVER LOVED
XXX

GRIEVING

I'm sitting there contemplating
My eyes filling up with tears
I remember all those memories
We shared over the years

As I lie there wide awake
I'm staring into space
The images in my head
Are of your beautiful face

I'm feeling empty, sad & lonely
Emotions I can't control
Feelings I've never had before
In my heart you've left a hole

Even though I know it's true
They say that I am grieving
I cannot help the fact
That I am disbelieving

I'm feeling so hurt
Feeling angry deep inside
You couldn't possibly imagine
How many tears I've cried

They say that times a healer
That you will start to be okay
I know that is not the truth
Whichever year or day.

EVERY DAY I STILL REMEMBER

The time is going quick
The years seem to fly
Every day I still remember
The day I said goodbye

You know I wasn't ready
It really broke my heart
Every day I still remember
How we're now far apart

When the sun starts to set
The moon starts to shine
Every day I still remember
How hard it is to be fine

You are really missed
You meant so much to me
Every day I still remember
How you made me so happy

You hold a special place
In our hearts & in our mind
Every day I still remember
How you were always so kind

You were a very special person
And heaven gained an angel
Every day I still remember
The loss of you is painful

I think of you with tearful eyes
Our memories I treasure
Every day I still remember
I will love you forever!

MIXED EMOTIONS

Feeling fed up & frustrated
With no reason as to why
Dullness inside of me
My eyes want to cry

Yesterday I was suicidal
Today there is a smile
It's like flicking on a switch
I've gone from feeling happy to vile

It's Friday 3pm
All I feel hopelessness
60 minutes will pass me by
Now all I feel is happiness

A dark cloud that follows me
It messes with my head
I've finally had enough with life
I think I'd better off dead

My head is under water
I feel like I'm about to drown
Nobody understands me
Is it a mental breakdown?

I want some attention
But when I get it, I've refused
I don't actually know what I want
I'm constantly confused.

THE REALITY OF MENTAL HEALTH

You put on a smile
You act like you're fun
Your thoughts run away
In your head you're all done

You say you're okay
You know it's a lie
You get into bed
Then that's when you cry

You think you're being stupid
There is so much frustration
So you start to drift away
Into a world of isolation

You're thinking way too much
About life and our society
All these thoughts in your head
But you know it's this anxiety

You can't shake it off
And it won't go away
Yet you get up every morning
And carry on with your day

You're constantly tired
You struggle to wake
You act like it's fine
But you know you're being fake

Falling asleep seems impossible
Horrible thoughts in your head
It always seems worse
When you're lying in bed

A heart that feels broken
Holding back all your tears
Standing and watching
Whilst your joy disappears

Why is this me?
Why do I feel so alone?
All these questions I have
But I don't like to moan

You're blind eyed
You're in denial
They start to ask questions
So, you run a mile

You feel so rubbish
Don't know what to say
It will all get better
You hope and you pray

The thoughts you think
Are they real?
Will you live for tomorrow?
Will this be your last meal?

Can't sleep
Can't stop thinking
Smoking too much
Too much drinking

Feeling like a failure
Maybe I took the wrong turn?
Your head starts to spin
Your heart starts to burn

Looking in the mirror
Staring at your face
All you are seeing
Is a massive disgrace

Swallow the lump in your throat
Wipe that tear from your eye
Think of something else
Don't you dare start to cry

My life isn't that bad
There're kids playing in the street
With a growling empty stomach
And no shoes on their feet

So why am I hurting?
Can't stop these feelings that I'm feeling
Depression go away!!
I need to start healing

Life is a lesson
Love & happiness we crave
We have to stay strong
Try to be brave

We can fight any battle
Our minds they can torture
I'm emotional, sensitive
And a dramatic over thinker

On my face I will smile
Inside it's so dark
My happiness has gone
There's no light without a spark

Declining offers to socialise
Using a lie for an excuse
Torturing yourself
It's the worst kind of abuse

It's time to speak up
It's now time to say
It's ok to get help
There is always a way

CAN'T SPEAK

When times are hard
When things are tough
When I can't let it out
When I've had enough

But you hold a special place
Held tight in my heart
That's why I feel down
When we are apart

The words I can't say
They don't seem to come out
I need you to know
I love you with no doubt

My love for you is real
I'm too scared to express
So, I'll do everything in my power
To try and impress

Please don't go
You will leave me devastated
It runs through my mind
Keeping me constantly frustrated

I'm crazy, obsessive
Too scared to get attached
So I'll isolate myself
Becoming really detached

Have a little patience
Be patient with me
Hopefully my words
Will start to flow free

MY HEART BREAKS

I'm breaking out in a sweat
Inside I am screaming
My fingers tightly crossed
I just hope that I'm dreaming

Then I remember those words
All those words that was said
The conversation we had
It's constantly stuck in head

They said "please take a seat"
I looked so confused
Why are they telling me
Such awful bad news?

I didn't want to listen
I didn't want to hear
The things she was saying
It was my biggest fear

"We're ever so sorry"
"We can't find a heartbeat"
My baby I love
I will never get to meet

A prince or a princess
I will never know
I will never get to see you fall
I will never see you grow

Why has this happened?
Why is life so unfair?
The flashbacks are torture
It's my biggest nightmare

I've cried so many tears
Full of heartbreak and sorrow
This feeling will never disappear
It will stay with me tomorrow

My pulse is racing
My heart beating so fast
My thoughts are driving me crazy
Constantly thinking about the past

Please know this little sweetheart
That you're my little treasure
I will think of you always
I will love you forever

OUR TIME WILL COME

We really want a baby
Little hands, little feet
We've tried for many years
It would make our family complete

We get a lot of disappointment
For every negative test
We hope it would be positive
It would simply be the best

It's such a hard thing
Struggling to get pregnant, Infertility
They say having a baby is hard
We are ready for the responsibility

It is the only thing we want
We hope & we will pray
Us being parents
It would definitely happen some day

The test will finally come back positive
It will be our little miracle
I will finally give birth
A baby so precious & adorable

Our time will surely come
We need to be patient and see
We'll finally become parents
A mommy & a daddy

JESUS, SAVE ME

Its 3am
I can't escape my mind
Driving myself crazy
Browsing trying to find

Why I don't know who I am
I don't know why I'm here
I'm feeling so empty
I'm really starting to fear

Somethings not right
I can feel it deep inside
I don't know what's the matter
I'm going out of my mind

I'm feeling really down
I feel like there's no hope
It's all getting on top of me
I am struggling to cope

I've started closing my eyes
Trying to escape the stormy rain
I'm praying and I'm praying
 "Please Jesus take away this pain"

I need you more than ever Lord
I'm standing over here
Please come and fill my heart with joy
Come down and take away this fear

I'm feeling so lost
My heart is broken out of control
I'm lonely and I'm drowning
I need you to come and save my soul

I'm down on my knees
I'm tired of feeling invisible
You can help me, sort me out
With you it's not impossible

Through my darkest times I see you
Because you are always there
Carrying me through good and bad
Because with you, you always care

I've got no more fight left in me
My strength has drifted by
So, I pray to you "Lord help me"
As the tears drip from my eye

WAITING ON GOD

The sun shines so bright
Through the branches of trees
Falling softly on the ground
These beautiful leaves

Its ever so quiet
So peaceful in the air
Silence all around me
So I open up in prayer

Jesus, please speak to me
Show me the right way
I'm waiting and I'm listening
I sit and I pray

I feel warm and content
A gentle breeze upon my face
Your love is so amazing
Your love I embrace

You've always got a plan
You saved me and I'm grateful
From happiness to sorrow
Your love is unconditional

Fill me up with hope and joy
Your good news is such a treasure
I will follow you until the end
I will worship you forever

THE LOVE OF GOD

His ears are always open
To listen to your trouble
He will never let you go
When you're going through a struggle.

When your mood is low
When you're down & depressed
He is always there to remind you
How much you're really blessed.

He forgives the worst sins
He shows unconditional love
Something that could only come
From the love of god above.

He's a father, king, messiah
No matter what he's always there
You know that you can pray for help
With god he will always care

He's the anchor that's keeps you on your feet
He picks you up when you have fell
He will help you to do your very best
He will help you to excel.

He will carry you through hardest times
Like footprints in the sand
He'll guide you through what is right
He'll be there to hold your hand

MOTHER

You've always been there for me
A shoulder when I'm down
With your sleeve you wipe my tears away
You change my upset frown.

You've always stood by my side
In every situation
You've always put me first in life
You have my respect and admiration.

You took me wherever I needed to go
You gave me all I needed
You have never let me down in life
As a mom you have exceeded.

You are amazing, wonderful & loving
You are definitely so much more
I love you more than you could possibly imagine
It's you who I adore.

Thank you, mom, for everything
Everything you've done & do
Brought me up & taught me well
I'm grateful for a mom who's you

You're the best mom ever
I'll love you until the end
Your heart is so big
You are my beautiful best friend

A WISE MAN

A wise man once told me
You have an active imagination
Use it how you need to
No need to give an explanation

A wise man once told me
Never put yourself down
You can be who you want
A lawyer, footballer or clown

A wise man once told me
If you can't be good, then don't get caught
He taught me how to love
Because love can never be bought

A wise man once told me
Always be yourself
Make sure your up in front
Never sit upon the shelf

A wise man once told me
Never listen to those mean
Never listen to the haters
Cos you're an absolute queen

A wise man once told me
Never cry over a lad
Put up your fists, fight back
That wise man I call my dad

BE KIND

Words are harsh
Think before you speak
Criticising others
On their looks or physique

We need to be aware
Start to be polite
We to start living
Live a life that's right

Feed the hungry
Clothe the naked
Help each other
Don't be persuaded

Let hate out your life
Help a pensioner cross the road
You are not a bad person
Let your love unfold

Start to be kind
Stop with the violence
Think before you act
Take a moment of silence

The world we are living
It's all guns and knives
Stop terrorising others
Stop taking people's lives

Take a look around
The world is magnificent
Change the way you live
Stop killing the innocent

Torture and murder
It's all heartache for families
The injured, the hurt
There're more hospital casualties

Take a little time to think
About the ones in heaven above
Because one day it could be
The death of someone you love

LIFE AS A CARER

We don't do it for the money
We do it because we care
We help them use the toilet
Brush their teeth & comb their hair

We help your family member
Make sure they have a meal
We love to hear their stories
That bond we've gained is real

We spend a lot of time with them
Lots of chats & cups of tea
Helping them to look their best
Now they're just like family

We sit with them when they are sad
We help when they are stressed
We try to make their day shine bright
We try our very best

We laugh when they are laughing
We greet them with a smile
A room of hearts full of love
That makes our work worthwhile

We put in long hours
All those hours on our feet
If by the end they feel so good
Then that's our day complete

We spend most of our time with them
Building memories forever
Helping them to feel content
Is something we endeavour

A BRIT'S 2019

Your headphones are in
The world is out
Your eyes are down
There's no one about

Your phones in your hand
There's no conversation
Tv's and phones
This is now our generation

Being healthy is expensive
Fast food is so cheap
A day on the Xbox
A boat load of sleep

Parents can't discipline
There's so much refusal
The world is obsessed
With the whole gender neutral

Brexit is crazy
Everyone turned vegan
We have lost all control
Do we really have freedom?

No more playing in the street
No more knocking on a door
Let's all go back
To 2004

CORONAVIRUS

The year of 2020
Thousands had died
An outbreak of coronavirus
That spread worldwide

A global pandemic
No more going into town
Everything was closed
As we went into lockdown

The shelves started to empty
Some were fighting, being mean
Bulk buying their shopping
Due to Covid 19

Weekly updates from the government
Watching the figures rise
It was heart breaking to watch
All those emergencies arise

Some still had to work
Some in 12-week isolation
Constantly washing hands
To try and save the nation

Nobody could believe it
How much it was a mess
So we started weekly clapping
To thank the NHS

We all followed guidelines
So we could start to thrive
We'll never forget what was said
"Stay indoors to stay alive"

THE EFFECTS OF FEAR

It's not a living thing
It's not even there
But lives in our heads
It makes us aware

Stops us from doing
Minds no longer clear
Takes so much from us
The thing we call fear

It takes away our breath
Leaves us paralysed
A mask upon the face
Our identity disguised

Like the beat of a drum
Heart starts pounding
Everything closes in
The walls that are surrounding

Sweat trickles down your cheeks
Words start to stutter
Hands & feet trembling
Stomach's got a flutter

It will take over our life
A head full of regret
Improve the way we think
Reform our mindset

So, don't hold back
Consequences are severe
Don't let it control you
The thing we call fear

BULLIED

He doesn't want to go to school
He wants to stay at home
He's sick of feeling hopeless
Fed up with feeling alone

They push past him in the halls
They nudge him with force
Spitting as he passes them
They never show remorse

Walking home from school
The way he always goes
He sees the bullies up ahead
His heart pounds, his body froze

He couldn't get the courage
So he turned the other way
He's tired of being beaten
Getting kicked everyday

He arrives home from school
His body all bruised
Fresh cuts on his face
He's constantly abused

He starts to write his note
"I can't do this anymore"
His life came to an end
He lay cold on the floor

YOUR STORY

This is your story
Do what you please
Be nice if you want to
Or be an absolute tease

Your life is your story
You are completely free
You can do what you want
Be anything you want to be

This is your story
Write it how you choose
You're in control
Whether you win or you lose

You are your own person
Write your own rules
Don't listen to negativity
Don't give your time to fools

You can surely be the best
You can always be on top
Always keep on fighting
Make sure you never stop

PUPPY LOVE

We need to change something
Something is missing
It doesn't feel like home
There's a place that needs filling

You came into our lives
We wouldn't change a thing
You're always happy to see us
So much happiness you bring

You are the cutest thing
The new addition to our family
You mean the world to us
You've settled with us perfectly

You're now at home with us
Bringing smiles & laughter
You make our home the best
You make our lives much brighter

You greet us with your love
You're now a part of us
We love to run around with you
And give you puppy fuss

I LOVE CHRISTMAS

Here comes Santa clause
Sliding down my chimney
I wake up Christmas morning
To find gifts that he has left me

I love the Christmas spirit
Drinking wine & eating cheese
Spending time with family
Whilst decorating trees

I listen to festive music
Sledding in the snow
I put my star upon the tree
Then kiss under the mistletoe

I build a snowman on my garden
I play with awesome toys
Singing songs as loud as I can
Making Christmas noise

I deliver Christmas gifts
To my family & my friends
I absolutely love Christmas time
I really hate it when it ends

Make sure that you behave yourself
Then Santa will appear
Happy Christmas everybody
Have a wonderful new year

THE LOVE STORY

They are both so young
Who never really spoke
Crossed paths at school
He would study & she'd smoke

They're 2 different people
They live totally different lives
He would play with sudoku
She would collect knives

They met at a youth club
And went on vacation
It started with a hello
It ended in deep conversation

They started to talk more
Slowly they got closer
They would text & meet up
Their bond only grew stronger

They became best friends
6 months after its official
They quickly fell in love
A love that was so beautiful

He took her to the London Eye
He had a wonderful surprise
When they got to the top
He looked deep in her eyes

He pulled out a ring
Then went down on one knee
Through his nervous voice
He said, "Will you marry me"?

Her eyes filled with tears
She replied with a yes
From all their adventures
This was surely the best

Both filled with excitement
They planned out the wedding
They both had each other
Which means they had everything

The wedding day arrived
The best day of his life
They both said "I do"
Finally, she is his wife

They've both got memories
Memories they will treasure
They're both deep in love
A love that'll last forever

WAIT AND SEE

I'm paralyzed with fear
Is there a way out?
Can anybody hear me?
I scream and I shout

I don't feel normal
I sometimes feel weird
Do people see me like that?
It's something I've feared

I have a sick sense of humour
Which people can't stand
But people don't like
What they don't understand

It's me, I'm still here
I have the same personality
Treating me different
Behaving irrationally

They look with a raised eye
They look at me and frown
Making me feel uncomfortable
I feel like I'm a clown

I know I can move forward
Be the best that I can be
They will never put me down again
Just you wait and see

WE WILL ALWAYS REMEMBER

The soldiers went to war
They fought for our freedom
They left their families behind
 For months they couldn't see them

So many marched away
Some men they sadly died
For us as a country
They stood and fought with pride

With a poppy bright & red
We'll remember them forever
How much they had to sacrifice
To make our lives much better

Time as passed but not grew old
In our hearts we hold them dear
We owe them thanks for their life
Everyday throughout the year

These men are true heroes
Because of them, we are free
So, wear that poppy proudly
For everyone to see

WHAT IS A FRIEND?

It runs through my mind
What does it mean to be a friend?
Someone who will always listen
Someone who will be there until the end

Someone who is by your side
Through good times and the worst
Someone who will always care
When your heads about to burst

Someone you can laugh with
Like you've never laughed before
Someone who will never be busy
And welcome you with an open door

Someone who will have your back
When you need a helping hand
Someone who can pick you up
When you can no longer stand

Someone who will love you
A friend is someone who is there
Someone you can tell anything to
All your secrets you can share

DRUG ADDICTION

It started with curiosity
Just a tiny little smoke
I'll only try it once she said
But taking drugs is not a joke

She started to smoke regularly
Then couldn't go without
She would constantly try to chase a high
But mainly she'd blackout

She really wants a better rush
So she started to inject
The addiction quickly escalating
Her body she'll neglect

The drugs taking over her life
She can't cope without a high
She hated herself for what she had done
Every night she'd sit and cry

She did it now to escape her pain
She felt ugly, sick and gross
She injected heroin one last time
Not realising she will overdose

She couldn't fight the addiction
She injected everyday
She lay there stiff, cold as ice
She had sadly passed away

A SILENT BATTLE

The body was found
Tied to the wood
Rope burns all over
Face covered in blood

A knife to the left
Glock 19 to his right
Could it have been murder?
Was it a fight?

No shoes were to be seen
His shirt was all torn
Was there anybody at home?
Any family to mourn?

There was nobody around
In his world all alone
Nobody to talk to
No one to pick up the phone

He abandoned his shoes
Sliced up his face
He needed to be free
He found the right place

He knew how to knot
Ripped his shirt in frustration
He couldn't pull that trigger
Couldn't give an explanation

No friends & no family
No children, no wife
So, he did what he had to
He took his own life

A GAME TURNED BAD

The sky was blue & clear
The boys went to the lake
A summers afternoon
They're on their summer break

An ordinary day
Boys playing games
It went terribly wrong
Ones gone up in flames

They took a can of petrol
Stole a light from their dad
They had no idea
It was about to turn bad

They were spilling out the petrol
Cos' this was just a joke
As they laughed, they lit the lighter
Then they saw a little smoke

The smoke it quickly escalated
It was spreading over his shirt
The panic it took over
Cos' he was getting badly hurt

He saw the lake of water
So he ran & took a dive
But it was too late for the lad
There was no chance he'd survive

Now there's nothing there
No body to identify
He left his family mourning
He left his family asking why

It was supposed to be just a game
Boys hanging out on summer break
Their silly & daft ideas
Have left their parents with heartache

A HIJACK GONE WRONG

She is running really fast
The wind on her back
Wrong place & wrong time
A victim to a hijack

With a blade to her throat
He took the keys to her Ford
She was only out cruising
Usually, she's in the house bored

The police on speed dial
Cos at night she's all alone
As she clicks the green button
He gets a glance at her phone

The worst mistake to make
Now she's running for her life
With a hooded fella chasing
Leading with the point of his knife

He finally catches up
Covered her mouth with his hand
She took an elbow to her skull
This was not what he planned

As she starts to wake up slowly
She muttered "how have I survived?"
But soon enough she realised
She's in a box, buried alive!

A KILLER

He's a psychopath, a killer
A man that nobody knows
He loves to kill & torture
He's living the life he chose

Adrenaline running through his veins
He spots a walker on her own
A grin upon his face
Now he's in his zone

He threw her down the alley
He dragged her on the floor
The victim shaking with fear
Feeling sick to her core

"You don't have to do this"
She pleaded with him, petrified
Her back against the wall
She begs for mercy, she's terrified

"I've murdered many people"
The killer confessed
Then looked straight in her eyes
He shot bullets in her chest

A puddle of blood
Stained on the street
Left her there lifeless
On the cold concrete

KILL OR BE KILLED

A stroll through the forest
It quickly turns extreme
It started off peaceful
Then he heard a loud scream

He seen a lady on her front
She's getting dragged by her feet
He hides behind a tree
He was trying to be discreet

Before he could make a call
A bag was placed over his head
He was chucked into a car
The worst was waiting up ahead

He was left on his knees
The lady mirroring in front
To the villain's it's just a game
He's the victim of their hunt

"Kill or be killed"
Now all he feels is guilt
He shot a bullet in her chest
It's her blood that's been spilt

He was forced to commit a murder
He couldn't cope with that pain
So, he shot the second bullet
He shot it straight through his brain

THE BREAK IN

He is walking through town
After a night with the boys
It's 3 in the morning
It's so silent, no noise

He is dragging his feet
Through the mist of the night
No traffic on the roads
There's no people in sight

As he stumbles round the corner
He approaches his front door
Looks down to find his keys
But notices blood on the floor

The door is slightly open
With a red trail to follow
His mouth is so dry
He is struggling to swallow

He's had too much to drink
The alcohol's messed with his head
As he crawls up the stairs
He finds his sister lay dead

he stood over her cold body
He realised she's been tortured
He's now the only child
The brother of that girl who got murdered

HER REVENGE

In a room so gloomy
So cold she sees her breath
Gazing into his picture
She is planning his death

Does she drown him?
With a knife take his eyes
Excruciating pain
She listens to his cries

She starts to carve nicely
Taking one limb at a time
With a smile on her face
It's the perfect crime

It's his final destination
He cannot escape
His screams are so silent
His mouths covered with tape

He's lost all control
Stuck in the worst situation
He slowly drifts away
Executed, in pure isolation

Lightning Source UK Ltd.
Milton Keynes UK
UKHW020744110121
376685UK00007B/197